MATHS 1

Home tests in basic mathematics

Understanding numbers,
computation, fractions, shapes
and tables

Roy Childs

Illustrated by Ken Smith

A Piccolo Original
Piccolo Books

Before You Start

This book is designed for your child to test his or her mathematical skills at home. A detailed introduction is given in the tinted pull-out section between pages 14 and 15. The answer key is also in this section. In case you want your child to work through the tests without access to the answers, you can pull out the tinted section carefully and keep it separate. (You may have to push the staples back slightly.)

So before your child starts work, turn to the middle section and read the suggestions on how to use this book.

Contents

Unit	Name	Description	Page
1	Understanding numbers	Notation, counting, place value	4
2	Computation	Addition, subtraction multiplication up to 3 figures	8
3	Fractions and sharing	Notation, addition, subtraction, division up to 2 figures	12
4	Shapes and angles	Names, symmetry, elementary volume and area angles	16
5	Measures	Length, area, time, money, weight	20
6	Understanding tables	Grids, tables, bar charts, scales	24
		A Note to Parents and Answer Key (Centre page pull-out)	i–iv
		Scores Table	28
		Maths Notes	inside back cover

Unit One

Write down how many apples in numbers and in words. The first one has been done for you.

Apples	Number	Word
🍎🍎	2	two
2. 🍎🍎🍎 🍎🍎🍎		

	Apples	Number	Word
1.	🍎🍎🍎		
3.	🍎🍎🍎🍎 🍎🍎🍎🍎 🍎🍎🍎🍎		

	Apples	Number	Word
4.	🍎🍎🍎🍎🍎 🍎🍎🍎🍎🍎🍎🍎		
5.	🍎🍎🍎🍎🍎🍎🍎 🍎🍎🍎🍎🍎🍎 🍎🍎🍎🍎🍎🍎		

Now write these as numbers.

Twenty-six 26

6. Thirty-seven ☐

7. Seventeen ☐

8. Three hundred ☐

9. Three hundred and six ☐

10. Four hundred and sixty ☐

Questions 11–15

Look at this number line. What number goes in each box? Box A has been done for you.

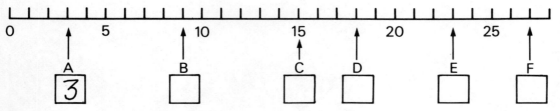

A = 3

Look at this train. All the carriages have a letter on them.

    Which carriage has 3 people in it?   B

16. Which carriage has 2 people in it?

17. Which 2 carriages have the same number of people? ☐ and ☐

18. How many people in carriage B?

19. How many people altogether in carriages A and B?

20. How many people in all the carriages together?

21. How many more people in carriage E than C?

22. How many more people in carriage E than D?

23. How many fewer people in carriage B than E?

24. Carriages A plus B have ☐ people in them.

25. Carriages A plus B have ☐ more people than carriage D.

Put in the missing numbers.

26.   27.   28.   29.   30.

Fill in the tens and units in the boxes below. The first one has been done for you.

tens	units
☐ ☐ ☐	☐ ☐ ☐ ☐
3	4

31.

tens	units
☐ ☐ ☐ ☐ ☐ ☐	☐ ☐ ☐

32.

tens	units
☐ ☐	☐ ☐ ☐ ☐ ☐

33.

tens	units
☐ ☐ ☐ ☐	☐ ☐ ☐ ☐

34.

tens	units
☐ ☐ ☐ ☐ ☐ ☐ ☐ ☐	☐ ☐ ☐ ☐

35.

tens	units
☐ ☐ ☐ ☐ ☐	☐ ☐

How many units in these numbers?

32 → [2] units

Question 36
34 → [ ] units

Question 37
58 → [ ] units

How many tens in these numbers?

31 → [3] tens

Question 38
46 → [ ] tens

Question 39
63 → [ ] tens

How many hundreds in these numbers?

214 → [2] hundreds

Question 40
786 → [ ] hundreds

Question 41
491 → [ ] hundreds

What does the underlined number stand for?

7<u>2</u>6 → [2 tens]

Question 42
7<u>3</u>6 → [3]

Question 43
4<u>6</u> → [6]

Question 44
1<u>7</u>4 → [7]

Question 45
<u>2</u>48 → [2]

Circle the correct answer. The first one has been done for you.

	Thirty-six	→	63	(36)	316	360	630
46.	Twenty-eight	→	20	82	28	208	280
47.	One hundred and twenty-two	→	122	121	212	102	112
48.	Two hundred	→	201	2000	202	200	220
49.	Two hundred and four	→	420	204	240	2004	402
50.	One more than 20	→	201	12	120	102	21
51.	Two more than 20	→	21	211	221	22	202
52.	Three more than 200	→	203	230	2003	320	2030
53.	Two less than 30	→	23	32	28	302	203
54.	One less than 100	→	101	110	91	109	99
55.	Two less than 282	→	280	284	262	82	28

Look at these numbers and answer questions 56–60.

523   736   452   276   1705

Which is the

56. biggest? ☐   57. smallest? ☐

58. Which number has a 3 in the tens column? ☐

59. Which number has a 2 in the units column? ☐

60. Which number has a 5 in the hundreds column? ☐

Unit One Score	Out of 60

Unit Two

Write the sum for each of the pictures by completing the boxes. The first one has been done for you.

   apples   pears   fruit
   [2] + [3] = [5]

1. [ ] + [ ] = [ ]
2. [ ] + [ ] = [ ]

Now fill in the boxes to make the sum correct.

3. [9] + [8] = [ ]
4. [10] + [5] = [ ]
5. [18] + [14] = [ ]
6. [27] + [33] = [ ]

7. [6] + [ ] = [14]
8. [ ] + [19] = [31]
9. [57] + [ ] = [107]
10. [28] + [ ] = [68]

11. 1 6 7
     2 3 1 +
     ———

12. 2 4 6
     3 4 5 +
     ———

13. 4 8 7
     5 3 5 +
     ———

14. Mike has 7 sweets, Greg has 4 sweets. How many sweets are there altogether? [ ]

15. Joan, Ali and Paul are 7, 6 and 10 years old. What do their ages add up to altogether? [ ]

How many more apples than pears?

　　　　　　　　　　　　　　　apples　　pears

🍎🍎🍎🍎🍎　　🍐🍐　　| 5 | − | 2 | = | 3 |

16. 🍎🍎🍎🍎🍎🍎　🍐🍐🍐　| ☐ | − | ☐ | = | ☐ |

17. 🍎🍎🍎🍎🍎🍎🍎🍎🍎🍎🍎🍎🍎　🍐🍐🍐🍐🍐　| ☐ | − | ☐ | = | ☐ |

Now fill in the boxes to make the sum correct.

18.　| 9 | − | 6 | = | ☐ |　　　　22.　| 63 | − | ☐ | = | 40 |

19.　| 22 | − | 12 | = | ☐ |　　　23.　| 31 | − | ☐ | = | 2 |

20.　| 49 | − | 17 | = | ☐ |　　　24.　| 86 | − | ☐ | = | 15 |

21.　| 100 | − | 50 | = | ☐ |　　　25.　| ☐ | − | 23 | = | 23 |

26.　　4 9 5
　　　 2 7 4 −
　　　 _____

27.　　3 8 4
　　　 1 3 8 −
　　　 _____

28.　　4 4 4
　　　 2 4 5 −
　　　 _____

29. John is 16. Matti is 7. How many years older is John than Matti?　☐

30. Ali has 24 marbles. Lisa has 9 marbles. How many more marbles has Ali got than Lisa?　☐

How many boxes are there?

   across down altogether
     $3 \times 2 = 6$

31. $\square \times \square = \square$

32. 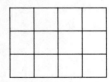 $\square \times \square = \square$

Now do these.

33. $4 \times 3 = 12$ 37. $5 \times 4 = 20$
34. $7 \times 4 = 28$ 38. $3 \times 12 = 36$
35. $9 \times 8 = 72$ 39. $11 \times 9 = 99$
36. $10 \times 5 = 50$ 40. $13 \times 10 = 130$

41. 1 2   42. 2 5   43. 4 2
   6 ×   9 ×   1 4 ×
   ―――   ―――   ―――
    7 2   2 2 5
                    4

                                   ―――
                                   ―――

44. The class has 4 rows of desks with 7 desks in each row. How many desks are there?

45. Barry is in school for 6 hours every day. How many hours is he in school over 4 days?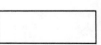

Now decide what is missing and write it in the box. The first two have been done for you.

```
   1 4              4 8
   1 2 [+]          1 6 −
   ─────            ─────
   2 6              3[2]
```

46.
```
   1 7
   5 [ ]
   ─────
   2 2
```

47.
```
   1 4 5
     2 5 −
   ─────
   1 [ ] 0
```

48.
```
     2 8
   [ ] 4 +
   ─────
     5 2
```

49.
```
     9
   5 [ ]
   ─────
   4 5
```

50.
```
   8 6
   2 7 −
   ─────
   5 [ ]
```

51.
```
     1 4
     4 ×
   ─────
   [ ] 6
```

52.
```
   1 5 9
   2 4 9 +
   ─────
   4 [ ] 8
```

53.
```
   1 5 3
       6 ×
   ─────
   [ ] 1 8
```

54.
```
   2 6 3
   1 [ ] 4 −
   ─────
   1 4 9
```

Now write in the answers below.

55.
```
   2 3 4
   4 3 7 +
   ─────
```

56.
```
   6 8 6
   2 9 1 −
   ─────
```

57.
```
   4 7
   8 ×
   ─────
```

58.
```
   2 0 4
   1 0 6 −
   ─────
```

59.
```
   2 6
   1 1 ×
   ─────
```

60.
```
   2 3 5
   1 5 ×
   ─────
```

Unit Two Score	
	Out of 60

11

Unit Three

Write what fraction is shaded below.

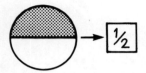 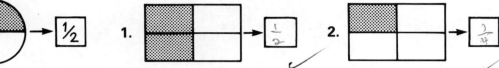 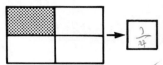

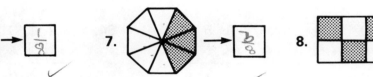

What fraction of each set of triangles is black?

 9. 10.

11. 12.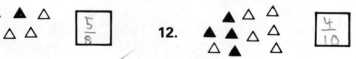

Look at this cake.

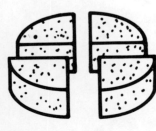

13. How many pieces of cake are there? ...... 4 ......

14. Write 1 piece as a fraction. 1 quarter

15. If you eat 1 piece what fraction is left? 3 quarter

Look at these apples.

There are 6 apples.
A line has been drawn around ½ of them.
½ of 6 is __3__.

Now do these. These triangles might help:

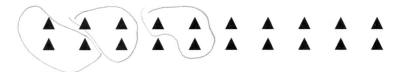

16. ½ of 8 is [4]   17. ¼ of 8 is [2]

18. ½ of 12 is [6]   19. ¼ of 12 is [3]

20. ¾ of 8 is [6]   21. ¾ of 12 is [9]

22. ⅛ of 8 is [1]   23. ⅜ of 8 is [3]

24. ½ of 20 is [10] 25. ¾ of 20 is [15]

Now do these. The first one has been done for you.

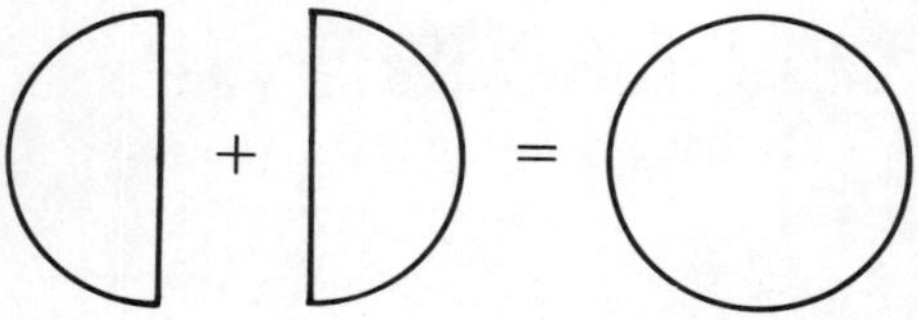

½ + ½ = $\boxed{1}$

26. ¼ + ¼ = $\boxed{½}$

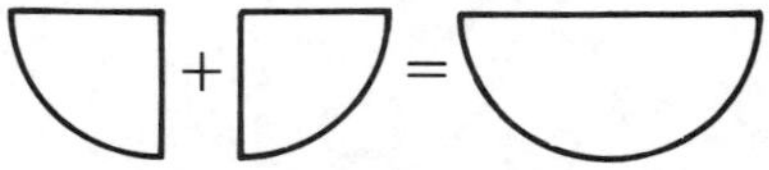

27. ½ + ¼ = $\boxed{3/4}$

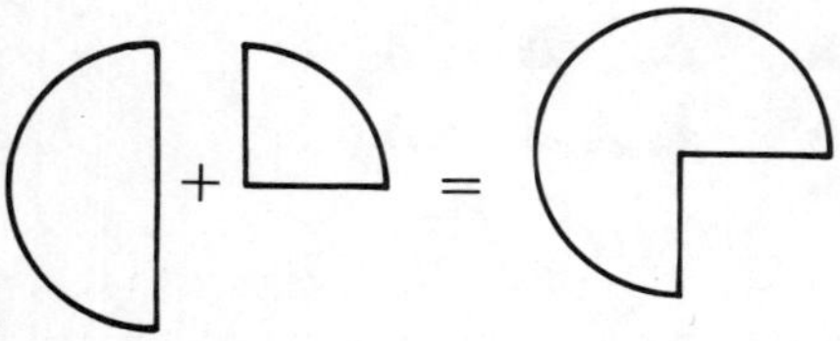

28. ¾ − ¼ = $\boxed{½}$

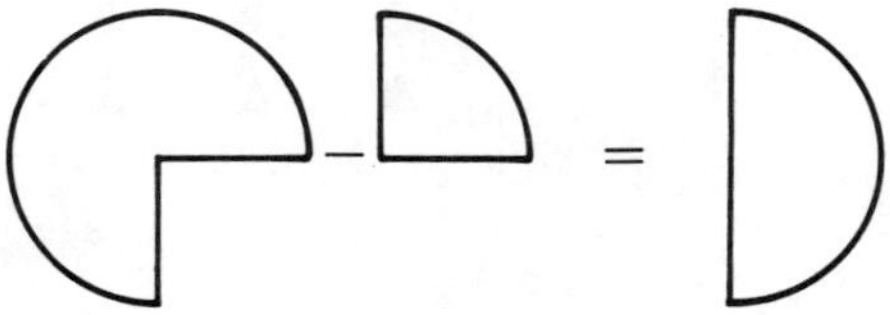

29. ¾ − ½ = $\boxed{¼}$

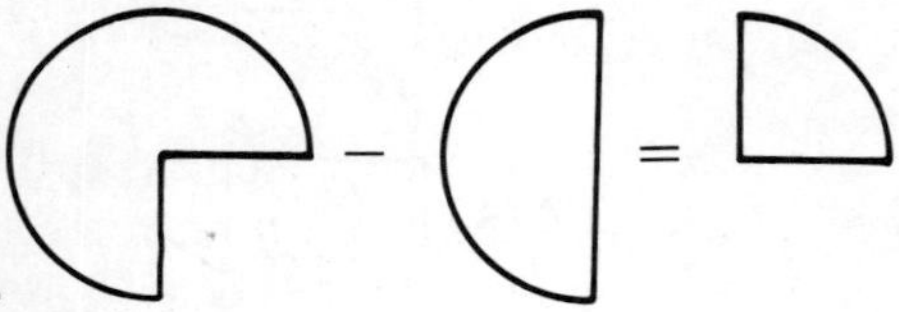

30. 1 − ¼ = $\boxed{¾}$

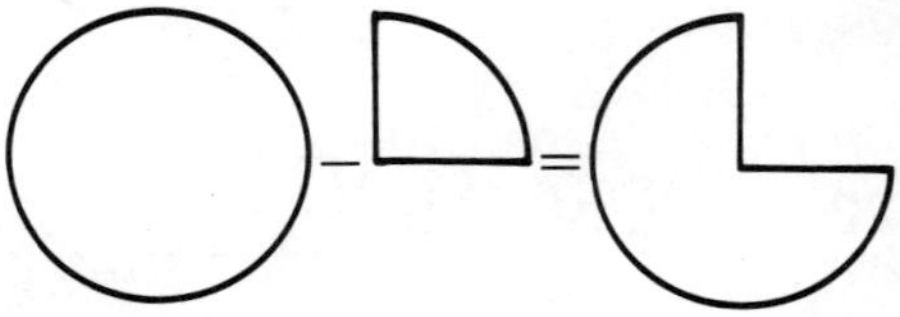

Now do these.

31. ¼ + ¼ + ¼ + ¼ = $\boxed{1}$

32. 1 − ¼ − ¼ = $\boxed{½}$

33. ¼ + ¼ + ¼ = $\boxed{¾}$

34. ¾ − ¼ − ¼ = $\boxed{¼}$

35. ¼ + ¼ + ½ = $\boxed{1}$

A note to parents

Important: read this before the child starts work.

About the tests
Each unit covers a different aspect of early junior mathematics. You are advised to go through the **inside back cover** with the child **before** he or she does the units. You should then sit with the child through the early units to make sure he or she knows how to mark the answers. It will also show you whether he or she is ready to tackle the rest of the booklet.

The units cover many topics which the child should have met at school. However it is unlikely that he or she has met everything in each unit. You will also find some of the questions in each unit are very hard. This is in order to challenge even the most advanced children. No one, therefore, is expected to get them all right.

You may mark the child's answers using the answer key on the next pages of this tinted pull-out. Alternatively you might like to let the child mark some of the sections him- or herself.

Getting the child started
Most children will need help in starting to use the booklet. As mentioned above, you should help the child and supervise his or her work — especially in the earlier units. Tests of this kind may seem a bit strange to him or her. Point out that, if the child doesn't understand, he or she can use the notes on the inside back cover. If these are insufficient, they can then ask you for further help. Remember that the tests are designed to tell you what the child can and cannot do so that you can help in those areas where he or she is having difficulty. Do not, therefore, tell the child the answer, but guide him or her to think about it. If this is insufficient, get the child to do some extra work before continuing with the tests (see below).

Also remember not to make the child over-anxious. The tests are a guide to help with further work and not a measure of what they must be able to do. Tell the child to take time so as to avoid making silly mistakes. It is best to tackle the units in the order presented in the booklet.

What to do when the child has finished a Unit
Use the answer key in this centre-page pull-out to tick each correct answer. The total number of ticks may then be entered in the score box at the end of each unit.

How to use the scores table on page 28
This is designed to bring together the scores for all six units. Those units showing the lowest score should be looked at carefully. Try to identify the particular area of difficulty.

What to do about low scores
No one is expected to get all the questions right. By looking at what the child has got wrong you might be able to see particular areas of misunderstanding which you can help to clear up. However, be careful, since children might have met the idea in another form at school. Ask the child to explain to you what he or she was thinking. Also have a look at his or her school work to get an idea of what the child is doing and how it is presented. Do not expect him or her to be able to do too much. Remember that mathematical ideas take a long time to develop. Children will learn part of an idea but be confused when they see it presented in a slightly different way. This is normal. What may seem like a very small

difference to adults can seem totally different to a child. Sometimes your explanations will be meaningless because the child is not yet ready to make that leap in understanding.

The best way to help the child is with patience and attention without driving too hard or expecting too much.

Further activities

No matter how well the child does, mathematical ideas need to be practised and developed regularly. These tests may have identified particular areas for further work. The other titles in the *Practise Together Series* (see inside front cover) will provide structured exercises with sufficient variety to keep the child interested.

Answer Key

Unit One

page 4		page 5		page 6		page 7	
1.	3, three	16.	D	31.	63	46.	28
2.	6, six	17.	A and C	32.	25	47.	122
3.	12, twelve	18.	3	33.	44	48.	200
4.	16, sixteen	19.	7	34.	85	49.	204
5.	23, twenty-three	20.	18	35.	52	50.	21
		21.	1	36.	4 units	51.	22
6.	37	22.	3	37.	8 units	52.	203
7.	17	23.	2	38.	4 tens	53.	28
8.	300	24.	7	39.	6 tens	54.	99
9.	306	25.	5	40.	7 hundreds	55.	280
10.	460	26.	10	41.	4 hundreds	56.	1705
11.	(B) 9	27.	12	42.	tens	57.	276
12.	(C) 15	28.	9	43.	units	58.	736
13.	(D) 18	29.	20	44.	tens	59.	452
14.	(E) 23	30.	18	45.	hundreds	60.	523
15.	(F) 27						

Unit Two

page 8		page 9		page 10		page 11	
1.	3+4=7	16.	7−3=4	31.	3×3=9	46.	+
2.	5+7=12	17.	14−5=9	32.	4×3=12	47.	2
3.	17	18.	3	33.	12	48.	2
4.	15	19.	10	34.	28	49.	×
5.	32	20.	32	35.	72	50.	9
6.	60	21.	50	36.	50	51.	5
7.	8	22.	23	37.	4	52.	0
8.	12	23.	29	38.	3	53.	9
9.	50	24.	71	39.	11	54.	1
10.	40	25.	46	40.	10	55.	671
11.	398	26.	221	41.	72	56.	395
12.	591	27.	246	42.	225	57.	376
13.	1022	28.	199	43.	588	58.	98
14.	11	29.	9 years	44.	28	59.	286
15.	23	30.	15 marbles	45.	24	60.	3525

Unit Three

page 12		*page 13*		*page 14*		*page 15*	
1.	$\frac{1}{2}$ or $\frac{2}{4}$	**16.**	4	**26.**	$\frac{2}{4}$ or $\frac{1}{2}$	**36.**	$12 \div 3 = 4$
2.	$\frac{1}{4}$	**17.**	2	**27.**	$\frac{3}{4}$	**37.**	$24 \div 4 = 6$
3.	$\frac{3}{4}$	**18.**	6	**28.**	$\frac{2}{4}$ or $\frac{1}{2}$	**38.**	2
4.	$\frac{1}{3}$	**19.**	3	**29.**	$\frac{1}{4}$	**39.**	3
5.	$\frac{1}{6}$	**20.**	6	**30.**	$\frac{3}{4}$	**40.**	5
6.	$\frac{1}{8}$	**21.**	9	**31.**	1 or $\frac{4}{4}$	**41.**	12
7.	$\frac{3}{8}$	**22.**	1	**32.**	$\frac{2}{4}$ or $\frac{1}{2}$	**42.**	18
8.	$\frac{4}{8}$ or $\frac{1}{2}$	**23.**	3	**33.**	$\frac{3}{4}$	**43.**	1
9.	$\frac{3}{6}$ or $\frac{1}{2}$	**24.**	10	**34.**	$\frac{1}{4}$	**44.**	7
10.	$\frac{2}{6}$ or $\frac{1}{3}$	**25.**	15	**35.**	1 or $\frac{4}{4}$	**45.**	3
11.	$\frac{5}{8}$					**46.**	5
12.	$\frac{4}{10}$ or $\frac{2}{5}$					**47.**	28
13.	4					**48.**	13
14.	$\frac{1}{4}$					**49.**	10 rem. 2
15.	$\frac{3}{4}$					**50.**	5 rem. 3

Unit Four

page 16		*page 17*	
1.	A	**11.**	A
2.	F	**12.**	6
3.	D	**13.**	12
4.	C	**14.**	C
5.	E	**15.**	3
6.	E	**16.**	2
7.	B	**17.**	B
8.	A	**18.**	5
9.	D	**19.**	8
10.	F	**20.**	4
		21.	8
		22.	6
		23.	12
		24.	12
		25.	18

page 18

26. 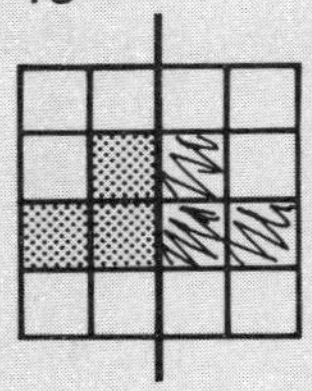 (3)

27. 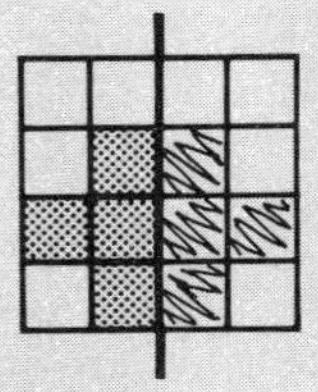 (4)

28. 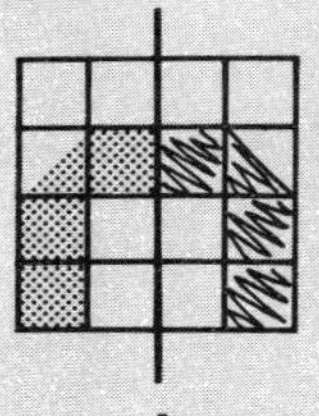 (3½)

29. 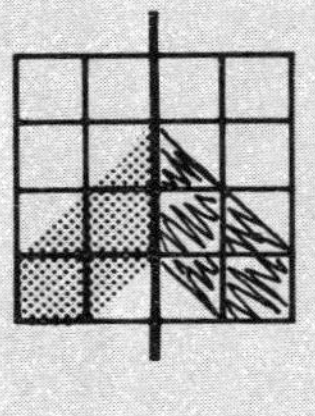 (3½)

page 19

31. car
32. bus stop
33. tree
34. house
35. N
36. 9
37. 6
38. 9
39. 3
40. 6

30. 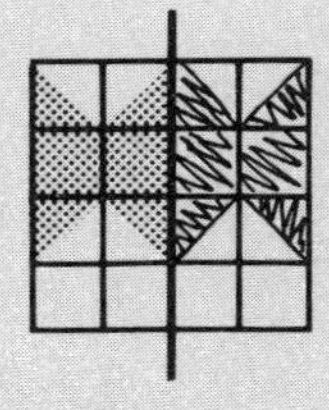 (4)

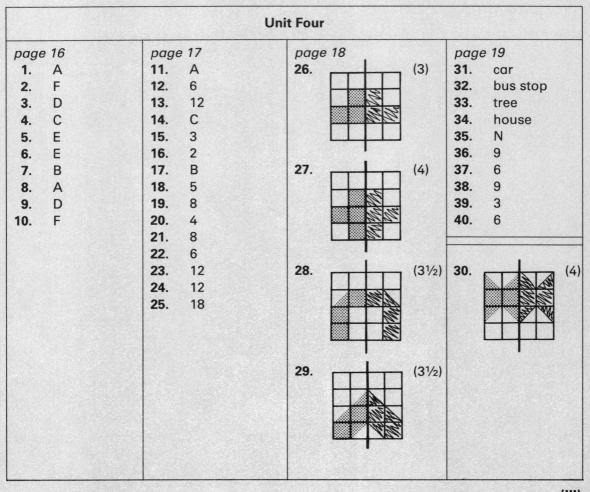

Unit Five

page 20
1. 8 cm
2. 2 cm
3. 20 cm
4. right angle (90)
5. 6.5 to 7 cm
6. rectangle
7. 8
8. 4
9. 11.5–12.5 cm
10. 8 shaded triangles

page 21
11. 4.00
12. 9.00
13. 5.45
14. 12.15
15. 12.45
16. 12.10
17. 12.25
18. 15 mins
19. 45 mins
20. 50 mins
21. 60 mins
22. 60 secs
23. 24 hours
24. 7 days
25. 365 or 366

page 22
26. 6p
27. 23p
28. £1.20 or 120p
29. £1.00 or 100p
30. £2.21
31. (sun)glasses
32. pen
33. 35p
34. 75p
35. 80p
36. £2.50
37. £1.55
38. £1.12 or 112p
39. £4.05
40. £4.40

page 23
41. less than
42. the same as
43. 200 g
44. 25 g
45. 75 g
46. 25 g
47. 1 sweet
48. 300 g
49. 1000 g
50. 40 sweets

Unit Six

page 24
1. Peter
2. Din
3. Gill
4. Ali
5. John
6. Jody
7. Jolene
8. 5 kg
9. 78 kg
10. 19 kg

page 25
11. March
12. 31
13. 4
14. 5
15. 30th
16. 18th
17. Thursday
18. Friday
19. 28th
20. Wednesday 19th March 1986

page 26
21. Wednesday
22. Tuesday
23. Thursday and Friday
24. 16
25. 10
26. 2
27. 10
28. 6
29. 3
30. 5

page 27
31. ⎫
32. │ Check
33. ⎬ the bar
34. │ chart
35. ⎭ drawing
36. 63
37. 50
38. 108
39. 58
40. 17

How many sweets each?

	sweets		girls		they each get
	10	÷	2	=	5
36.	12	÷	3	=	4
37.	24	÷	4	=	6

Now fill in the boxes to make the sum correct.

38. 8 ÷ 4 = 2
39. 12 ÷ 4 = 3
40. 25 ÷ 5 = 5
41. 36 ÷ 3 = 12

42. 2 ÷ 6 = 3
43. 19 ÷ 19 = 1
44. 49 ÷ 7 = 7
45. 45 ÷ 15 = 3

46. 3)15 = 5
47. 3)84 = 28
48. 7)91 = 13

49. There are 32 sweets to be shared between 3 people. How many do they each get and how many are left over?

they each get	left over
10	2

50. A game needs 5 players in a team. A class with 28 children can make how many teams?

number of teams	left over
5	3

Unit Three Score	
	Out of 50

Unit Four

Look at this train.

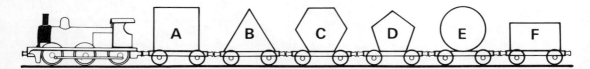

The carriages are shapes. What letter is inside the

triangle B   3. pentagon D

1. square A   4. hexagon C

2. rectangle F   5. circle E

The shapes below are to be folded along the dotted lines. They will then look like *one* of the shapes A, B, C, D or E at the bottom of the page.

Match the folded shape with one of the bottom ones. The first one has been done for you.

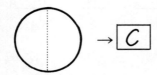 → C

6. 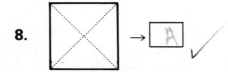 → E

7. 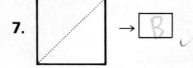 → B

8. → A ✓

9.  → D

10. 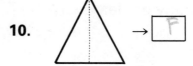 → F

A   B   C   D   E   F

Look at these shapes A, B and C. Imagine picking them up.

    A   B   C   D

12. It has 6 faces

11. The cube is shape A

13. It has 12 edges

15. It has 3 faces

14. The cylinder is shape C

16. It has 2 edges

18. It has 5 faces

17. The pyramid is shape B

19. It has 8 edges

Look at these shapes:

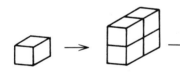 → 4   The big one is made from 4 little ones.

How many little ones are these shapes made from? Sometimes you can only see part of one.

20.  → 4   21.  → 8

22.  → 6   23.  → 12

24. 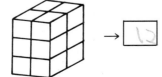 → 12   25. 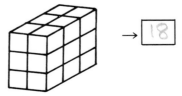 → 18

Shade in the mirror shape. Then write the number of squares you have shaded in the circle next to it. The first one shows you how.

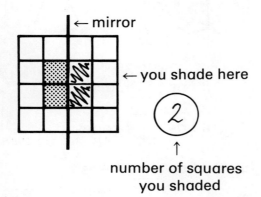

26.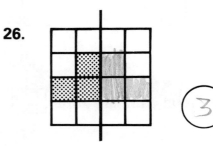

27.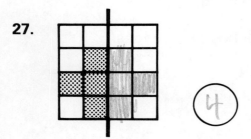

28.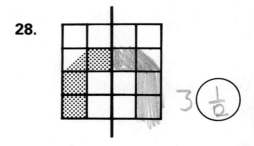

29.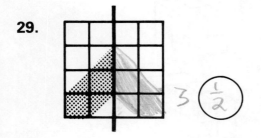

30.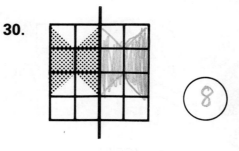

Look at the man in this picture. Use the compass to answer these questions.

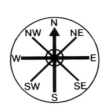

	In what direction is the man facing?	N	Ⓢ	E	W	
31.	What will he see if he faces East?	(car)	cow	bus stop	house	tree
32.	What will he see if he faces West?	car	cow	(bus stop)	house	tree
33.	What will he see if he faces North East?	car	cow	bus stop	house	(tree)
34.	What will he see if he makes a ½ turn?	car	cow	bus stop	(house)	tree
35.	In what direction will he then be facing?	(N)	S	E	W	

Look at this clock. The hand always starts at 12 and is turned to point at another number.

What is that number if it makes a

¼ turn clockwise [3]

36. ¼ turn anti-clockwise [9]

37. ½ turn clockwise [6]

38. ¾ turn clockwise [9]

39. ¾ turn anti-clockwise [3]

40. 1½ turns clockwise [6]

Unit Four Score	
	Out of 40

Unit Five

Look at this rectangle and triangle.

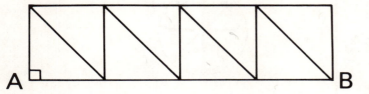

You will need a ruler.

1. Measure the length of the above rectangle. — 8 cm

2. Measure the width of the above rectangle. — 2 cm

3. Work out how far it is all round it. — 20 cm

4. What is the angle at A? — 1 right angle

5. Work out how far it is all round the shaded triangle. — 7 cm

6. Which covers more area – the shaded triangle or the rectangle? — rectangle

7. How many shaded triangles are needed to cover the rectangle completely? — 8 triangles

8. How many right angles are there in a square? — 4 right angles

9. Use a piece of thread to help measure the length of the above line. It is ____ cm long

10. Shade in a shape that has the same area as the rectangle above.

Write, in figures, the time on these clocks.

 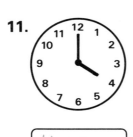 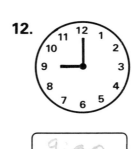 

11. 12. 13.

3·00   4:00   9:00   5:45

14.    15.    16.    17.

12:15   12:45   12:10   12:25

18. On clock 13, how many minutes until 6.00?   15

19. On clock 14, how many minutes until 1.00?   45

20. On clock 16, how many minutes until 1.00?   50

21. How many minutes in an hour?   60

22. How many seconds in a minute?   60

23. How many hours in a day?   24

24. How many days in a week?   7

25. How many days in a year?   365

How much are these coins worth together?

= 5p

26. = 6p

27. = 23p

28. = £1.20

29. = £1.00

30. = £2.21

Look at this shop window.

31. What is the most expensive thing?

    £3.45

32. What is the cheapest thing?

    pen

What change do I get?

50p → pen → 30p

35. £1 → pen → 80p

33. £1 → comb → 35p

36. £5 → hat → £2.50

34. £1 → chocolate 25p → 75p

37. £5 → glasses → £1.55

Now do these:

38. 90p
     22p +
     ─────
     £1.12

39. £1.45
     £2.60 +
     ─────
     4.05

40. £2.71
     £1.69 +
     ─────
     4.40

22

Look at these scales.

Scale A   Scale B   Scale C

Now complete these sentences or answer the questions.

5 sweets are __more than__ 100g.

41. 3 sweets are __less than__ 100g.
42. 4 sweets are __the same as__ 100g.
43. 8 sweets weigh __more than__ 100g.
44. How heavy is 1 sweet? 25 g
45. How heavy are 3 sweets? 75 g
46. What weight must you add to SCALE A to balance the scales? 25 g
47. How many sweets must you add to SCALE B to balance the scales? 25
48. What weight will balance 12 sweets? 300 g
49. How many grams in 1 kg? 1600 g
50. How many sweets make 1 kg? 40

Unit Five Score	
	Out of 50

Unit Six

```
Rows
A  |    |    |    |    | Sean |
B  |    | Ali|    |    |      |
C  |    |    | Roy|    | Gill |
D  |    | John|   | Din|      |
E  |Peter|   |    |    |      |
     1    2    3    4    5
```

Look at this grid. There are children's names in some boxes. We can find the names by looking at the rows and columns.

Who is in column 5 and row A? It is Sean. Write the name for each of these.

    5A **SEAN**　　　　　　3.　5C Gill

1.　1E peter　　　　　　4.　2B Ali

2.　4D Din　　　　　　　5.　2D John

Look at these people standing on some scales.

40 kg　　　35 kg　　　46 kg　　　32 kg

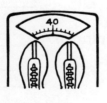　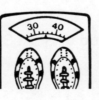　　

Bill　　　　Ali　　　　Jody　　　Jolene

6.　Who is the heaviest?　　　　　　　　　　Jody

7.　Who is the lightest?　　　　　　　　　　Jolene

8.　How much heavier is Bill than Ali?　　　5 kg

9.　How heavy are Jody and Jolene together?　78 kg

10.　How much heavier are the 2 heaviest than the 2 lightest?　19 kg

Look at this calendar.

March 1986	
Monday	3 10 17 24 31
Tuesday	4 11 18 25
Wednesday	5 12 19 26
Thursday	6 13 20 27
Friday	7 14 21 28
Saturday	1 8 15 22 29
Sunday	2 9 16 23 30

11. What month is it? — March

12. How many days in the month? — 31

13. How many Fridays are there? — 4

14. How many Mondays are there? — 5

15. What date is the last Sunday? — 30th

16. What date is the 3rd Tuesday? — 19th

17. Jody's birthday is on the 20th. What day is that? — Thursday

18. Jill's birthday is 8 days later. What day is that? — Friday

19. What date is that?

Day	Month	Year
28th	March	1986

20. If Bill's birthday is on the 3rd Wednesday, write it out in full.

Day	Month	Year
19th	March	1986

This bar chart shows how many children came to class during one week. There are 20 in the class when everyone turns up.

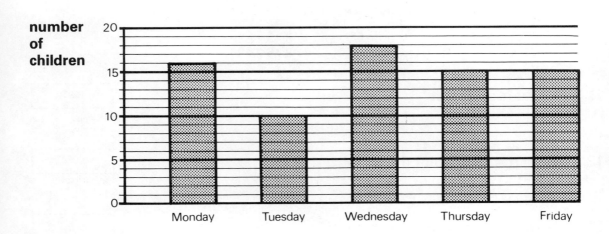

21. On which day did most children come? Wednesday

22. On which day did fewest children come? Tuesday

23. On which two days did the same number come?

    Thursday and Friday

24. How many children came on Monday? 16

25. How many children came on Tuesday? 10

26. How many people were away on Wednesday? 2

27. How many people were away on Tuesday? 10

28. How many more children came on Monday than Tuesday? 6

29. How many more children came on Wednesday than Thursday? 3

30. How many days was the class not full? 5

This table tells you how many days we had of each kind of weather in 1947.

RAIN	100
SUN	63
CLOUD	80
WIND	50
SNOW	8
MIXED	64

31–35
Draw a bar chart to show what the table tells us here. The rainy days have been done.

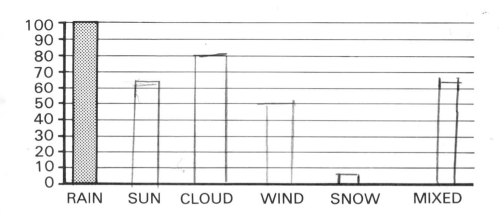

36. How many days had sun in 1947? 63

37. How many days had wind in 1947? 50

38. How many days had rain or snow? 108

39. How many days had wind or snow? 58

40. How many more cloudy days than sunny days were there? 17

Unit Six Score	
	Out of 40

Scores Table

Unit One	UNDERSTANDING NUMBERS (Notation, counting, place value)	Out of 60
Unit Two	COMPUTATION (Add, subtract, multiply up to 3 figures)	Out of 60
Unit Three	FRACTIONS AND SHARING (Notation, add, subtract, divide)	Out of 50
Unit Four	SHAPES AND ANGLES (Names, symmetry, volume, area angles)	Out of 40
Unit Five	MEASURES (Length, area, time, money, weight)	Out of 50
Unit Six	UNDERSTANDING INFORMATION (Grids, tables, bar charts, scales)	Out of 40
	Total	Out of 300